Cardinals

by Elizabeth Neuenfeldt

BELLWETHER MEDIA • MINNEAPOLIS, MN

Blastoff! Readers are carefully developed by literacy experts to build reading stamina and move students toward fluency by combining standards-based content with developmentally appropriate text.

Level 1 provides the most support through repetition of high-frequency words, light text, predictable sentence patterns, and strong visual support.

Level 2 offers early readers a bit more challenge through varied sentences, increased text load, and text-supportive special features.

Level 3 advances early-fluent readers toward fluency through increased text load, less reliance on photos, advancing concepts, longer sentences, and more complex special features.

★ **Blastoff! Universe**

Reading Level

Grade K

Grades 1–3

Grade 4

This edition first published in 2022 by Bellwether Media, Inc.

No part of this publication may be reproduced in whole or in part without written permission of the publisher. For information regarding permission, write to Bellwether Media, Inc., Attention: Permissions Department, 6012 Blue Circle Drive, Minnetonka, MN 55343.

Library of Congress Cataloging-in-Publication Data

Names: Neuenfeldt, Elizabeth, author.
Title: Cardinals / Elizabeth Neuenfeldt.
Description: Minneapolis, MN : Bellwether Media, 2022. | Series: Blastoff! readers : Backyard birds | Includes bibliographical references and index. | Audience: Ages 5-8 | Audience: Grades K-1 | Summary: "Developed by literacy experts for students in kindergarten through grade three, this book introduces cardinals to young readers through leveled text and related photos"– Provided by publisher.
Identifiers: LCCN 2021000670 (print) | LCCN 2021000671 (ebook) | ISBN 9781644874912 (library binding) | ISBN 9781648343995 (ebook)
Subjects: LCSH: Cardinals (Birds)–Juvenile literature.
Classification: LCC QL696.P2438 N48 2022 (print) | LCC QL696.P2438 (ebook) | DDC 598.8/83–dc23
LC record available at https://lccn.loc.gov/2021000670
LC ebook record available at https://lccn.loc.gov/2021000671

Editor: Betsy Rathburn   Designer: Andrea Schneider

Printed in the United States of America, North Mankato, MN.

Table of Contents

What Are Cardinals?

Cardinals are medium-sized **songbirds**. They are part of the cardinal family.

All in the Family

rose-breasted grosbeak

painted bunting

scarlet tanager

Male cardinals have bright red feathers. Females are mostly brown.

female

male

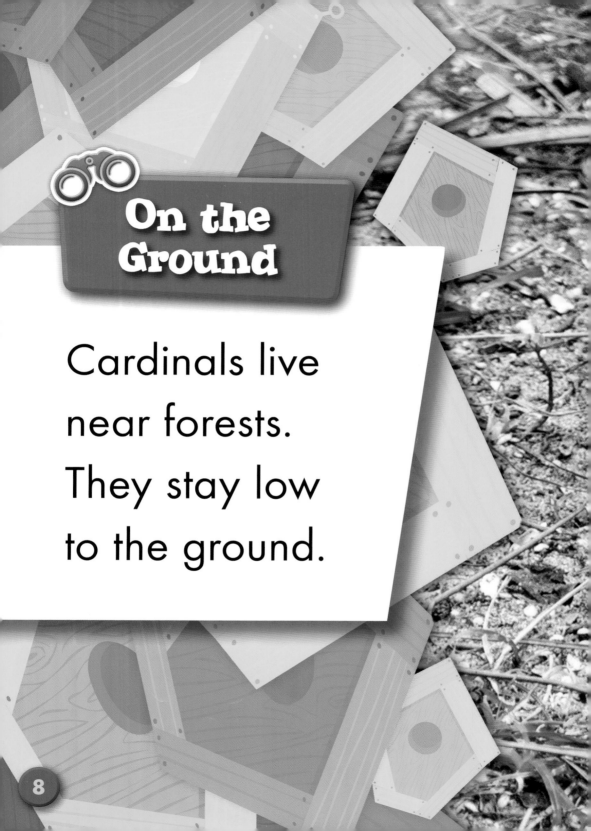

On the Ground

Cardinals live near forests. They stay low to the ground.

Cardinals build nests in low branches and **shrubs**. Their nests look like cups.

nest

These birds find food near the ground. They eat seeds, fruit, and **insects**.

insect

Cardinal Food

seeds

fruit

insects

13

Singing in Pairs

Cardinals sing together. Songs help males find **mates**.

Cardinal Call

Cheer!

Cheer!

Cheer!

15

Mates live together in spring and summer. Females build nests. Males bring them sticks.

mates

Cardinals live in **flocks** in winter. They look for food in groups.

flock

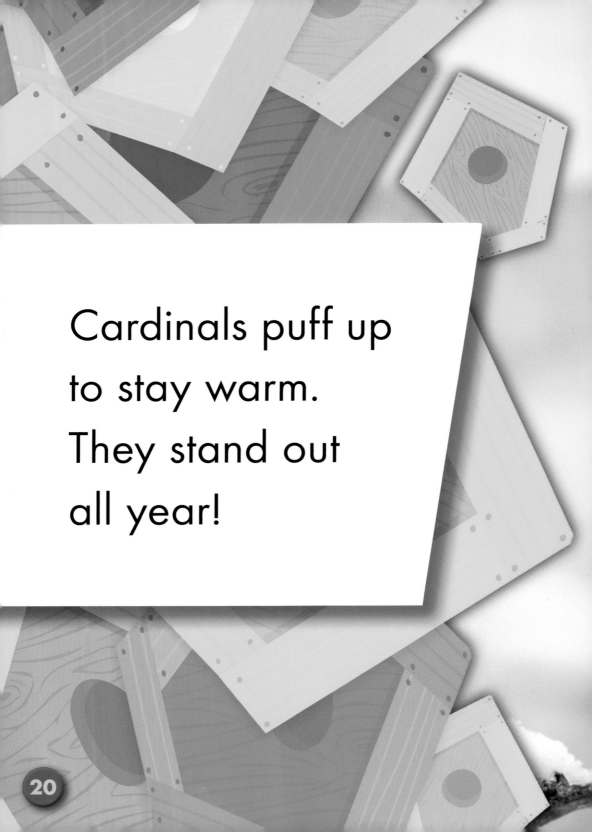

Cardinals puff up
to stay warm.
They stand out
all year!

Glossary

flocks

groups of birds

shrubs

bushes

insects

small animals with
six legs and hard
outer bodies

songbirds

birds that make
musical sounds

mates

partners

To Learn More

AT THE LIBRARY

Nilsen, Genevieve. *Cardinals*. Minneapolis, Minn.: Jump! Inc., 2020.

Opie, David. *All the Birds in the World*. White Plains, N.Y.: Peter Pauper Press, Inc., 2020.

Statts, Leo. *Cardinals*. Minneapolis, Minn.: Abdo Zoom, 2018.

ON THE WEB

FACTSURFER

Factsurfer.com gives you a safe, fun way to find more information.

1. Go to www.factsurfer.com.

2. Enter "cardinals" into the search box and click 🔍.

3. Select your book cover to see a list of related content.

Index

The images in this book are reproduced through the courtesy of: Connie Barr, front cover (cardinal); Wang Jui-Lin, front cover (background); RLS Photo, p. 3; Danita Delimont, pp. 4-5; Jayne Gulbrand, p. 5 (rose-breasted grosbeak); Matthew Orselli, p. 5 (painted bunting); FotoRequest, p. 5 (scarlet tanager); Bonnie Taylor Barry, pp. 6-7, 22 (mates); Gerald A. DeBoer, p. 7 (female); Bob Silverman CDN, pp. 8-9; Cathleen Wake Gorbatenko, pp. 10-11; Sally Thornton, pp. 12-13; AN NGUYEN, p. 13 (seeds); Ollga P, p. 13 (fruit); Kerli Kaljur, p. 13 (insects); markusmayer, pp. 14-15; William Leaman/ Alamy, pp. 16-17; Tom Uhlman/ Alamy, pp. 18-19; Harry Collins Photography, pp. 20-21; Rizwan Mian, p. 22 (flocks); Marko Rupena, p. 22 (insects); irra_irra, p. 22 (shrubs); rodmacpherson, p. 22 (songbirds); Daryl Haight, p. 23.